Thoughts And Other Human Tendencies

Reneltta Arluk

BookLand press

Published by BookLand Press
15 Allstate Parkway, Suite 600, Markham, Ontario L3R 5B4
www.booklandpress.com

Printed and bound in Canada.

Library and Archives Canada Cataloguing in Publication

Arluk, Reneltta
Thoughts and other human tendencies / Reneltta Arluk.

(Canadian Aboriginal voices series)
Poems.

ISBN 978-1-926956-14-5

I. Title. II. Series: Canadian Aboriginal voices series

PS8601.R52T56 2012 C811'.6 C2012-901228-9

Canada Council for the Arts / Conseil des arts du Canada
ONTARIO ARTS COUNCIL
CONSEIL DES ARTS DE L'ONTARIO

We acknowledge the support of the Canada Council for the Arts, which last year invested $154 million to bring the arts to Canadians throughout the country. We acknowledge the support of the Ontario Arts Council (OAC), an agency of the Government of Ontario, which last year funded 1,681 individual artists and 1,125 organizations in 216 communities across Ontario for a total of $52.8 million. We acknowledge the financial support of the Ontario Media Development Corporation for our publishing activities.

"Poetry is constructed out of
remnants found in ruins."

~ *Based on Milosz' premise*

Table of Contents

Once Were

It's not like the dream I told you
yesterday when I was dying in my
sleep.
And it's not how I cried suddenly
no explanation left at hand.

I guess the best way to explain this
one is
that it's like the eagle feathers I
have, they once flew.

Connection

Do I know how to be my blood?
Do I have cultural portrayal?
Do you love me from across the gravel road?

Regurgitation

I wonder if the British
Who fled their country of oppression and royal ruling
Thought North America would become the new anarchy,
Only to discover their own humanity
Was knowing how to rule.

Chiasmus

We can only strive from what we are given
And strive for what we are not given.

(About the hardships of living)

Indian Time

Stand alone, kicking stone, hurting my toes on the Keepers of the Past. Mother bead me a story of dandelion wine and copper rings; of how my land of heroes was destroyed to lost… perhaps dead… Spirits.

I'll make us some tea with honey with bannock and jam. I'll pretend to braid the hair you don't have because it's styled like mine, not long like my dreamed warriors. Maybe Mom I learned too much in school, maybe Mom I'm not traditional enough for my Indian warrior… maybe Mom I'm White.

Teach me my ways that I could be strong for myself, I need to be alone, to learn my past, to be in the now, to be a woman, to be myself.

So I'll tell my dreamed warrior, yes; I loved you once but you were just a picture in my mind, and you haunted me for years. So now you decide to come, Indian time, I shake my head, torn apart, deep emotion, would I know you if you knocked on my Hamlet door… what can I tell you? I've been waiting.

Still-life

When I slept in that bed alone
I slept so well.
Haunted by your eagle feather, still
Connected to mine.
My life still.

Afterthought

i used to write in the dark
to feel my thoughts and not let the eye
try to alter what i see
after the thought

Contradiction

in all life's journeys
we fall to reach the sky and touch the ground
in that moment
we are contradiction at its finest

To a Man Sitting in Whitehorse, Yukon

This old man is sitting on a cement corner
facing the sun
looking over the cityscape
at the clay cliffs.
He is thinking of his life gone past
hunched over he remembers when
he was young, when he used to dance
for his grandmother and how she used to smile.
He loved to make his Kookum smile.
He smoothes his hair under his hat
and puts his hat back on,
pulls at his scraggly beard.
She used to wear these moccasins, he remembers
the soles had been patched many times over the years,
the beautiful brightly coloured beads
so tightly sewn into a flower design had lost a few threads.
When she was younger, she used to dance with him too,
sometimes she'd sing…
He breathes a song to remind himself of her Love.
Minutes go by where he doesn't move,
just sits there
then reaches for this paper bag, all crumpled
the top rolled into a handle,
he pulls it close to his body,
waits a moment,
takes a breath.

He stands up and walks off into the direction of the sun.

Fly-fisherman

Hey old man with your Tilley hat,
Where are all the fish?
Not on the sidewalk by the post office.
It's a bit nippy out today. Are the fish biting?
Do you care?

Hey old man where'd you get that hat?
From your fly-fishing daughter, didn't she catch the
   trophy winner?
Doesn't she hobby her own flies?
That's okay old man, it looks good on you,
That's all that matters.

An Inuvialuit Children's Song

As taught to me by my great-aunt Martha Harry

Da-bee-dow
Ralung-na
Ana-yu
Ralung-na

Ook-tik-tow
Ralung-na
Mo-mik-ho-lau-ru-la-runga-a-hey-a-a-a-yay

Com-na-nay
Nat-tan-bay
Ana-yu
Ralung-na

Ar-look-taw
Ralung-na

Mo-mik-ho-lau-ru-la-runga-a-hey-a-a-a-ya

(All transposed in my crazy phonetic code)

Four Colours of Thought

I come to you from the Emotional place and I
    carry myself with me
And I bring my tears

I come to you from the Historical place and I
    carry myself with me
And my Grandmother's and Grandfather's teachings

I come to you from the place of Song and Dance and I
    carry myself with me
I, too, can hear the sound of the drum

I come to you from the place of Meditation and I
    carry myself with me
The power of thought from the eagle's point of view

The Writer

With pen in my hand I hold a thousand dreams
    left without a happy ending
    or maybe there are   but I will never tell.
Hey there do you want some company?
    Yeah I got a great shadow, it does whatever I do
I call it my assistant   although it doesn't do much
    Just what I do in an imaginary sort of way
    It has no name like peanut butter
    The possibilities are endless.
"I can do what you do," it says to me
    but what would be the point.

Fringes

Inspired by a young dancer who sees colour only in her beads and fringes

When I was little my mother sewed, by hand, my first fancy shawl outfit. It was blue and purple with fringe. My dad took me out on the Pow-wow trail for the first time, new outfit in tow, showing everyone in the land my shiny outfit. How I loved to dance!

As the years grew on, my outfits changed shape and colour. My mother always made them and never once complained. She used to watch me practice in the basement, dancing to the tapes recorded from the Pow-wow before.

One spring, my father grew ill and we knew that he would not be able to take me on the Pow-wow trail that coming summer. I was devastated. I was getting taller, and was beginning to get noticed by the judges. Would no one see my hand-beaded Cree flower with purple and red outlined in black? And my new moccasins, real tan this time! Women on the reserve taught my mother the beautiful technique. We were so proud.

It was decided that my mother would come with me this time. I knew the road and the best places to camp. At last, she could watch me dance on real ground.

We arrived at the first Pow-wow of the season. The energy was high, bells along with feathers were bustling everywhere. We heard the announcer calling, "Fancy Shawl!" I rushed my mother to hurry and get my braids done and make sure my feathers were in perfect order.

I told her to set the chairs up in the front of the bleachers, where we dancers sit. I ran ahead as Mom gathered the blankets and chairs to watch me dance for the first time. As we dancers picked our starting spots, I saw her enter the arena and I got excited. I knew I would dance strong for her.

The song began and I began to jump and twist, fringes twirling, drum beat heavy, voices pitched high.

Mid-dance I noticed a woman telling my mother she couldn't sit in the front, pointing to the bleachers where she was permitted to sit. You see. My mother is White, my father Cree.

I continued to dance as I watched my mother move further and further away from me. I danced higher and harder.

Outer Shell

Listening to the rain, feeling the cool moist breeze
Naked, crying for the false reality that we create
Yet break before we are swallowed into plastic.

Death Unanswered

Saw the wind begin to drift the snow
Gone to no man's land
Driving past the blizzard's eye
Going to better pastures

Last night breathed the air of many
Saw no difference from last week
Last year I spoke to your father (fate)

He said that death was knocking on your door
I guess you weren't answering,
I guess he didn't persist.

Open Wound

Be the cat sneaking in my window
Through my heated heart
Lapping up the blood spewing
From the open wound called vulnerability.

Yellow Eyes

Looking into the darkness
Imagining these eyes looking at me
From there
Open
Yellow
At me
I appear in the light looking at them
Praying the light never goes out
But the light doesn't follow me
I have to stay within it to be free
But I know that is not freedom
I am contained.

I do not want the yellow eyes to step into the light
As much as I do not want to step into the dark.

Rain vs. Thunder

Sometimes rainfalls and
thunder shake the sky and
they scare people, sometimes.

But other times they're exciting.
Well what I feel is neither.

I feel sad not for thunder,
but for rain.

Torrent

In terrible danger
The river flowed.
Winds are fire
The river flowed.
Took lots of acres
The river flowed.

Poetic Magnets at the San Francisco Airport

Dream Rain, Bright Summer
She was very delicate
Kind cry, White fire, Style

Inhalation / Exhalation

Less on me breath on you
More on you breath on me

The Rain Took Off

~ **Ben Doig**

If the lightening catches the dog house
We will have no more dog
Maybe we will see her bones
Who will chase the chickens?

Shut in

Against the snow
    the blizzard
Alone
Well. Well. Well.

Good Shot

through the
blizzard's eye
I saw the sun
and when I
blinked there
was a gun
it fired towards
the frozen moon
it shot the
star that fell
and here I am
a fallen angel
in the snow
a snow angel

Purified

So Jesus died at 33
Resurrected into Spiritual Release
Became pure again
Pure again

Broken Man

Long time passed when I couldn't face the mirror in fear of what I would see, although I've probably seen it before, since lives are lived after all for death.

Rivers rushing to its eternal fall over the now smoothed terrain, thirty feet to its doom. Fish squandering down below searching for prey to kill. Darkness overcasts the sun so long that one can start to believe that it is all that exists. After all what can one believe if not able to see the whole truth, well one side.

I never found the broken man in the woods. Like everyone said, there were only traces of broken bush and dirt tracks; perhaps he wanders or am I walking in circles again?

The wind blows through the trees tickling them with their own leaves creating small tornadoes in abandoned caves where bears once dwelled until the beast of greed took over our souls and felt the need to feed off the compassion of material wealth instead of mind. It is such a harsh thought to feel numb, to no longer feel pain. Or is it pain we always feel, that there is nothing left past that.

I live in the woods in a cabin far from heckle and immune to control and power. I can't be told what to feel when I know in my heart that I am lost. That I cannot be me in a world that is farthest from knowing who they are. I am not here anymore… I am not me anymore… I am no longer real…

Irony

It's surreal this feeling, it is like I am simply watching my body, that part of my spirit has left and hovering over and around me but it is not there.

Like my spirit is feeding my mind little ideas and my body is accepting them, non-changing in reaction.

In fact, I am the opposite of reaction. I am de-action, I am de-motion, except for the loss of feeling, that ironically enough, I feel.

Thought Number 249

I'm curious about why I am here;
Perhaps I am meant to jump out of an airplane…
But really I wake up before seven a.m. at ground level.
Oh well, it's all relative to the fact that I'd rather fly.

What I Saw in Mexico

I saw the drug people at the border on our way to
Puerto Vallarta
I saw one man in military regalia carrying his child
with his wife walking along the side
of the road.

I saw the Manzillo cemetery with its cement painted
white and Jesus on top,
Arms reached out to save all, crosses all white.

I saw the water and its many colours of brown, dark
blue and aqua.
Its calmness and its white surf crashing amongst the
rocks in its way and on the beach
leaving behind polluted remains.

I saw why Jack Kerouac stayed.

I tasted food so simple and pure that the flavour
refreshed you and filled you in ways you
can never forget.

I felt the hot sun in Mexico on more than one
occasion, and I loved it.
It was in control of my skin's fate and I got burned.

I heard the sound of the waves crash, the iguanas
    rustle, the fan wind us back the recycled
heat we gave off, the sound of a refreshing shower
    being turned on calling to me.

I heard words alien to me but did not feel alienated.

I called my Spirit to join me in Mexico.

She loved it too.

Suicide Prevention

How to prevent suicide:

Smile

Make eye contact

Don't ignore your neighbour, he could be next

Talk to a distant acquaintance if the opportunity arises

Don't assume someone else is doing better than you. It just may not be the case.

Offer your ear, more than once if necessary.

Propose an out, yourself!

Don't be greedy.

Kindness

Genuineness

Communicate.

How did this happen?
This solid foundation (supposedly)
Cracked
Action to kill self
Sounds hard to swallow
Yet, it happens. Action to kill self.
To cease, to live no longer, for what reason would one justify?
To allow the idea and then follow through.

What happened?!

I saw you recently, we chatted
I was kind and made eye contact
I should have offered a number
An address,
Anything.
Communication.

I'm sorry that Death's call was stronger than Life's.
I hope you're ok now.

Hester Fester

I feel like suicide is contented-flavoured candy
Pass me another cigarette
Pass me another killer idea
Death is passion. Dying is a vacation spot.
Can I handle being abused any longer?
Two days is eternity it lasts too long for the hell I am feeling inside.
I can feel the welling evil seething below the love, bubbling to rush the system.
I am inexpressive for there is no such thing as debate.
I am ready now to explode.
Are you compulsive? Are you there?
Do not intrude on me. Leave me to the dogs.
Hester Fester laughing bums.

Mistress Death

The mysterious woman in black
Faces the window, I cannot see her face.
All in black,
Down to her three-inch clog heel.

Blackness

I never saw the sunlight you know
The very thought of shining scared me
I envy your need to fly away to where nothing
  touches your soul.

Last night when I was crying I saw the mirage
A being coming down from somewhere
She told me that I am black
Black. Black. Black.
That I was as dreary as the ink in my pen
I was as lost as the stone thrown into water.

Am I around? Are you thinking of me?
Want to taste the thought of cheesecake in my mouth
Oh, what the hell.

The wicked never understand the damned
The good never want the ugly,
Masterminded journeys through the pits of depression
Render all ideas of pleasure to a halt.

See you later big boy
So long to the charm you possess
May fog cover your agility
No longer shine, be mine.

Standing in Water

we look at the world we live in
and falter at its size
that when I stand and look at you
I can see through your disguise
if I stood to see you long enough
I'd see into your eyes
and I'd be left unknowing and asking myself why
why do we stand in water to our knees
and keep looking at the sky

Self-Portrait

If there is a time when I swallowed too much water
This would be the time to drown

I am up in the air but falling
I am beauty underneath this fog of self-pity
I am truth under a lie yet am truth no matter what

I am naive yet so aware it is far beyond my age
I am love
I'm love
I am love and appreciation for what it is I have

Mister can you help me
I lost a bit of my dream last night when I thought I
heard your voice but I was mistaken
I was misunderstood perhaps I was known too well

I love you I want to understand you
I can hear you scream

I love the life you lead, be lead, be
Temperature is set at the shoe faith

Fork in the Road

It wasn't too far down the broken path
that I felt unlikeness
But it was too much to handle at the time
I wanted you to love me too

I Cope

1.

When the moon shines in the light,
with delight
it creates the wisdom within
the marching band of hope
I cope.
Leftover merry weather feelings
ceilings.
Damn the blessed sun
son of a gun
I hear the dreaded sound of reality
In last year's time
there is a rhyme, chime, nakedness and godliness no
longer hand in hand.
I demand.
Relentless emotion go soothingly into this goodnight,
be light,
Should I be the one to sorrow over light?

2.

Ten years gone, be done, oh death kill me
rude down the earth with the thought of
happiness going into sin I love you
with all charm and bearing ground be the start
of eternal beginnings within.
In death there is no beginning
having left the thought of solemn thoughts.

I forgive you, do you forgive me?
Which of course is the ideal of my demise!
Tender, cherish to the creations of the time when I
kissed you with no regrets
I wonder if there is life beyond the horizon.
Just to let you know that I love you
Just a thought to tell you I sin within
with anxious thoughts and unforgiving sames
I hope to understand the future with the past of
blurry days.
To you I lend the helping hand of reality.
Never let go of tomorrow's realization that one does
not succeed
with sorrow
but helplessness,
I love you
I tend to believe in fate, not hate
Let there be a sensuous hand to which I can relate.
So good-bye, good knight
Be there a son in my growing womb that tenderizes
the day
that belongs to the only one who can surely sooth
the uneasiness I feel, to which all I feel is black.

Lady May the Glass Be Broken

Listen, listen to the chime of time
Do you hear it? Can you taste the tale?
For you see there is nothing to hear
Only to feel

Lady may the glass be broken
So that your bloody finger drips
Into the memory of long ago
Telling you tales like comic strips

I saw you, did I tell you
Or did the wind blow it softly in your ear
A deafening aroma left lingering
For memories don't disappear

Surrounding
Surrender darling breathless and sincere
For there lies a coveting knife in my hand
Words spoken to the taste of your tongue
There is isn't much of anything
When all is said and done

Exposé

I was left there to smoulder like the remains of a
burned-up matchstick.
No longer useful except to collect in a dusty ashtray.

I had no glory and she had no shame and between the
both of us
we were gutless heathens revolting from the sun.

I was once a martyr of stone whose monument
resembled
that of Henry V of England with his wily eyes and
wig hair
if either existed on him, I am terribly unsure.

But one thing I remain sure of is her lack of shame
led me to believe that the world was in hiding
and she was the exposé.

Conspiracy

"Is there a conspiracy against Kerouac?" he asked.

~ Jack Kerouac in a biography by Anne Charters

1.

Yeah, is there?
He is so confused and underlined
a line going everywhere but nowhere in the same.
Like me, lost, wandering, wondering where to next?
What life to be leading, be.
Saw my soul once, felt reality lightly, gone,
like the sun in December, left, a linger… memory.
A grave is made for my soul today lost and not found, yet,
like Jack. Drowning in the sorrow of life, majority rules
are so hard
when minority is right, I'm right, the world is wrong.

2.

You know what's wrong with the world, space, space is being used for the wrong thing, materials, clothes, and trends, now it's coffee shops, beatniks and shoes, a lot of fuckin' shoe stores.

People worry about money too much, what can I own, what do I have in the bank, people rush too much, walk fast, drive fast, impatient, and fake people. I'm generalizing but majority rules.

How good do I look? I look good, I'm not watching you, but I am, the silent-movie camera rolls, I am acting, you are acting, chameleon, friend to foe, foe to friend, do I know you?

Money is bullshit, banks are a business investment, modernize, computerize. Computers are de-socializing the world, don't talk to me, look at screen, type, download, chat line, sex is cyber, physical closeness is disease. No war, not yet, but we recycle glass and plastic, we drink bottled water.

Do drugs, don't smoke, save $, invest, wear DKNY. I wear Doc's, Doc's were created by a Nazi, child slave labour. Racism, Colors de Benetton, dramatize, shock, be subtle, be a man, be a feminist, it's ok to be gay, wash your fruit - it has pesticides, we have suicide, mothers killing their children, we only want boys, commercialize, murder is cool, violence rocks.

I am part of the X-generation, rapid movement, coffee is small in Paris, hair is gross, small people no longer exist, small x, medium is small. Where are we going, overpopulation, everyone is rude, I hate my hair, I hate groups of girls, they're evil. Men... men…

Advertising

"Insert here," says the hole
"Play safe," says the box
"No glove, no love," says the billboard
"Insert here," says the hole

The Player

I knew you loved me once, twice
Between two slips of sheets
Too bad you had to run along
And play with the rest of the girls

The Musician

It's your show, play me, play hard,
You're funky, you're cool, don't stop
the rhythm, don't kill the time,
          Faster player, keep the beat.
Mercy man, be the band…

And at that time my inspiration
stops playing the harmonica.

Dreaming of Jeannie

Sitting here, listening to two girls talk.
A guy in front of me collects thousand dollar bills.
How I wish I knew where he lived, wondering where
he keeps his money.
I think he's the type of person who stashes his fill in a
pillow or between the mattresses
Or is that where he keeps his S&M material.
These two girls are bothersome,
I just whiffed a perfume scent that reeks,
suffocating my nose.
The waitress at the Gold Range is a hard-looking
woman, could be 26 looking 31.
She wears her hair up high like "I Dream of Jeannie."
Does she want men to recognize her as that, I dream
of Jeannie?
Gee, Miss, you remind me of the lady in the lamp.
I dream of Jeannie, I dream of you.

The One-Night-Stand Among Friends

Largely in life we play the game of survival
Succumbing sometimes to, sex
It's harsh seeing life unfold in an unpredictable destination
What will occur later on? Where will I be led, or am I the leader?
Always being the cool chick until you sleep with one of the guys.
Then there's that, will-I-still-fit-in thought.
Getting caught the morning after is always the strangest.
You come strolling out of his bedroom in your wool socks and tee and underwear
and there down the short hallway is his good buddy looking at you saying "hi"
nonchalant but inside wants the details, and he gets them.
Welcome to the one-night-stand among friends.

With this turn of events many directions can be followed.
The one and only night with "Oh my god that will never happen again!"
The occasional drunken embrace leading to more short morning hallway meetings,
Or lastly, the friendship has become love and pure attraction.

This lasts until the summer is over because the sun
    creates a pure happy feeling in all and
during the dark winter the only thing that keeps
    the relationship going is sex and the
occasional high while watching a movie.

Travelling, Fucking, Drinking

1.

"I love you."
"Yeah, I know you do."

What does that mean? Does it mean I know you love me, so stop trying to show it, relax, fucking calm down. You're not going to save me, this is not your battle, let it be. "Call you tomorrow." Will I?

Are you in a bar right now drinking or are you outside my hotel, barred out, thinking not of me, but needing me near so you can think because only I can stir emotion in your heart. Or are you at home sitting at the table writing with Raspberry Schnapps sharing secrets with your pen, finally able to express yourself. Do religious thoughts please you? Does X mark the spot?

Now you laugh freely at the world, out mockery, subduing your inner emotions, hell they came out to no one, to me. You don't know what I'm going through, do you. Talking in your language, who cares since I don't understand. Yeah I know you love me. Yeah. So we're going out tonight so I can watch you not getting drunk, fuck who cares if you read this, if you don't.

I'm fucking upset, crying on a whim. I need you right now, I don't need you explaining why I'm upset to someone else, I don't need to sleep in a fucking hotel,

I don't need to be told to be social, how can I fuckin' be social when I can't even be myself. Nothing here is mine. Not even you. Lying there, reading, hiding in the bathroom for 20 minutes. Hiding what? I wonder about you and your ability to handle liquor. Do you hide from me?

You are scared, you are overwhelmed sometimes, but that is all right. You push me against a post, you are looking at me, I am screaming at you my thoughts, "I'd do anything for you, I'd love you, I'd take away your pain!" You stare at me for 30 seconds as I reply, screaming, and you scoff, release me and say, "Let's go."

Fuck, go where?

2.

"I don't know, I haven't been drunk in a long time."
"Well now, what are you thinking in?"
"I'm not drunk."
"You had one bottle, I'd be drunk."
"Two, and I'm not drunk."

He slurs in Spanish, in English, staggers, his nose red, his eyes half-aware of the world around him. Maybe he likes it that way, half-aware, then you'd only have half the regrets, half the worries of why we are here on earth. I'd give you my fuckin' soul for you to see what I see. Then you'd feel no need to blur your sanity, depth, drowning. Slapping my face by the taste of another fermented grape, raspberry, sweet desire, to world retire.

I know you ache and feel like time, bored, routine, unfocussed on the purpose of life, fuck. Reality. "I love you, are you drinking?"

Half fantasy, or is it all, don't worry about hurting my feelings, don't melodramatize the scene. Fuckin' be yourself, be nothing if that's what you are, I still love you, you're untamed. You're wild and I won't take that from you. But I don't want you to die. Fuck I know it's hard when you see more than the world, step back as you see simplicity, see Lego men building Lego worlds.

But face it, we're there and there is innocence to be found. That is the foundation of tranquility, and if you don't have it find it in something else.

3.

"What look is it that I give you? What look?"

You know, playing the funny man on booze only lasts until there's nothing funny about a man on booze. You want to fuckin' die, don't live cuz you're afraid of what your family will feel, if you want to fucking live, live for yourself, love for yourself, give love for your wanting to love someone else, don't fucking do it if you can't face the only thing that has answers. Don't drink wine. "Don't whine." You are so brilliant you know, how you pick-up on things, how aware you are, but sometimes you are wrong.

I hold your arm cuz I'm in love with you, I never did before cuz I wasn't, I can't get enough of you, when I lean into you I'm aroused, I feel my body come, in emotion, when I feel your back, my breasts fit to you, feel it? When I run my fingers through your hair it is ecstasy.

Looking Glass

Perhaps I forget the moment when I stopped walking on eggshells; or I forgot when I stopped remembering that I've always been. I can't recall the last time I knew what was going on within myself. It's my subconscious; it's all in there someplace, the real me, where I truly exist. I've been told that others can see the real me inside. Only glimpses though, only glimpses. I'm just curious to know who I'm trying to be then. I guess that's where the inner conflict happens, the boundary between me and the real me, the one I can't even see. You know he asked for all of me and then I forgot who she was. It's not what you see that affects me; it's what I realize in myself. It's the reflection in the self-proclaimed mirror.

Saints and Liars

Sometimes the violence surrounds me.
I know I'm not the only one
but in the course of history violence always ends in death
and I'm not wanting to die…

It seems the only people who live forever are
saints and liars.

Savour

Still bring the gaze, haze, maze of my mind and cravings. Stand to your left and move to your right. No sleep just sweat and being wet. Sex is the time I love the most, and you're the host. Music baby indeed it is, on my body, bite on my ear, your arms wear the marks of too many beers.

All I can savour, all I can say if this is food then give me my portion today. If this is the end I want to go backwards. If this is the top then let me fly. If this is the game then deal me in. If this is the colour then paint me thick. If this is the number then give me your pen. If this is the door then goddamn it let me in. If this is the moment I'll hold my breath. If this is the vortex then let me stop time. If this is the star then let me be led. I'm the whiskey in your Pepsi. I'm the cinnamon on your breath. Life is the lucky and time is your repeat. When the air makes its frost I'm the one that wipes you off. Pay the man for your seven-dollar drink and let's get the fuck off the stage. I want to make your heart race with the words on this page.

Velocity

Gin and tonic, please (ahem)
Soda and lime and lemon water

I love sex, y'know the carnal kind
Where the intensity is felt in the muscles and
expressed in the eyes.
Where your mouth never closes because it is too busy
gasping with each thrust.
Yes that kind of sex.
The kind where it can last two hours or twenty
minutes, which does not really matter
because either way you're left satisfied, gratified,
satiated and sweaty.
Ahhh, where was I? Yes, René. She's a hell of a gal
with the motivation of a speeding
train that's always going somewhere and sees no
reason to stop.

Tormented Tormentor

I love to hear the thundering sound of a slap across
the face and the torment it creates.
So easily it is to dismantle the tranquility.
So hard to get it back.

Social Media

In the midst of a power failure
And everything seems natural, no buzzing or electric
shock-waved energy
Just people talking, laughing and yelling
Relying on their natural ability to converse
No longer depending on TV or a favourite song.

HOW MANY PEOPLE ARE BORED RIGHT NOW?

One Liners

/Do you Love me? She asks with the fate of no man.

/I guess I could have kissed your lips when you left me behind.

/It's hard to feel life between your toes.

/Sometimes I Love you, but how can you Love selfish ego?

/Maybe if I would play the fool, but why be something you are.

/Will we share a room tonight or will I be sacrificed for cheaper rates?

/No I've never seen you before. Perhaps I've been around but not with you.

/Remember when I heard the gunshot. How you leapt up and I fell.

/Is a one trick pony and today is doing her tricks for free.

Isis Sisi Yes Yes

Your rich dark skin
So strong and healthy
Sensual and thick
I smell your strong scent that
Matches the colour of your skin
Like deep earth, dark and moist.
        There I go being a lesbian again
        I thought it wouldn't happen
But then I met you and knew instantly
That you were special and that perhaps
I want to touch you, to feel your skin
Next to mine and taste your mouth
See what it has to offer
        Your eyes are so beautiful and young
        Your face so challenging,
        Beauty and intelligence, maybe
Isis, you are.

Lunch Break

So you say, you're a dreamer.
But here, I see you in the day leaning against the old
  wooden building with two dollars to
your name, unfazed.
I say, I am a writer, as I stand in my conservative
  black oxford shoes with my ten minute
hair-do.

So he asks what I'm doing,
I answer with "lunch break."

He's not the dreamer wishing that someone will take
  him away from this nine-to-five job,
That this one poem cherished will bring him
  recognition being left aimlessly around,
wishing to be discovered.

He's not a dreamer, I am.

Golden Harps and Silken Threads

I saw the dreamer last night
He said that you were lost
And that maybe I cried silently
alone not wanting anyone to see

But the shadow whispered
to the wind that rain came
from my eyes and so betrayed
up went my disguise

The dreamer told the envious
moon of my horrid stream and
mocked my feeble strength by
tickling the stars to twinkle
as I sit on the porch to tire

Well the dreamer cried to the
heavens that I was not to be
alone and angels appeared with
golden harps strung with silken thread

And they played the loveliest tunes
but like the dreamer said
my dreams had turned to puddles

So there I was awoken
with eyes puffy, and sad
some dreams come true
and that's too bad

Sittin' Blue

Sittin' in a fancy restaurant
Looking at a Valentino suckin' on a Schnapps
Never needed any reason to say I was sorry
Haven't felt the need to run
But what can be said here
Lyin' in the sun

CHORUS:
I want you to know my love is fair
It broke in a thousand pieces and you don't care
Remember when the story all came true
Now you're gone and I am sittin' blue

Lyin' by a side of the road leading to nowhere
Eating fried potatoes
Watching men watching women watching the birds
fly around
Like the sound of a beating heart
Lost the thunder in the rain
Can't control this feeling
It's coming back again

CHORUS

Last night was the greatest
I never felt such high
If only this emotion could keep me satisfied
I lost my patience he left with the sun

And now I sit here wondering how it all came undone
My hand trembles in fear
My eyes flutter when the air is clear
My life is passing I am staying
I can no longer control
This is reality
This is not me
I guess what will be will be

CHORUS

Thinking that I lack self-control
Wondering if it's you I want to know
Early in the daytime I am blue to you
I can't behold what is known, lost my soul

BRIDGE:
I want to tell you that I'm through
I can no longer be loving you
I wonder if it's sadness or if it's pain
But all that I know is that I can't go through this again
I guess I'll put together what is left
Pick up all these pieces
Drop all this garbage
And move on

CHORUS

After Bar Conversations

Is that a milk tin?	Blake
Yes, it is	René
Yeah, it's Arabian	Doug
From Australia	Doug
What kind of milk?	Blake
Ostrich milk?	Wing
No, no Australia	Doug
I don't know what kind of milk, cow!	Doug
Aborigine milk	Blake
Right from the tit!	Blake
Goat milk?	Wing
It's definitely Iranian	René
From Australia	Doug
What's on the label?	Blake

(All you can see of the label on the tin, that's on top of the fridge, is "Re...cow milk")

What are you guys talking about?	Aaron
The milk on top of the fridge	René
What's that say?	Wing
Retired cow milk	Blake
Refrigerated cow milk	Doug
Is it Russian? It looks Russian	Wing
Retired cow milk	Doug
Grab it; let's take a look at it.	Blake

(Doug goes and gets the tin)

RED COW MILK!	All
It must be Russian	Blake
The writing and the Red Cow	Wing
See, there's the Australian symbol	Doug
That looks like Russian writing	Blake
Red Commie cow milk *(pointing to the tin)*	Wing
I like my cows black and white man	Blake
What's it good for?	Wing
It can be used for baking, cooking	Doug
Here, let's open it and take a look at what this stuff looks like.	Blake

COOKIES! Blake/Doug/Wing

(All hands go into the tin at once)

To My Bro

He jumps, twists, plays gravity's adversary.
Repeats lost moves to grasp the glory.
Just once.

He trades two feet for one with four wheels.
He is the ramp king,
He can do anything.

Love: Your Sister

A Scene for a Movie

Married family.
Father away from home, on the phone to the
youngest or younger older child.
Mom and dad had a fight sometime prior to this call and
mom is feeling sorry,
vulnerable, close by, listening to the girl talking to daddy.
She is standing, possibly doing dishes.

"Mom! Dad said it's your turn to keep track of the hurts…"

Young girl goes back to the phone listening.

"…He can't keep count anymore."

Balancing Act

Simple Pleasures
Simple Life
Husband Man
Woman Wife
House Cable
Phone Strife

Simple Pleasures
Simple Life

The Moment in Between

Sitting on the edge of their seats
Waiting for the next laugh
For the next wave of humour.
Hesitance is the sweet silence before the roar.

How Trees Were Created in New Mexico

Many years ago, near a place named San Pueblo, roamed many buffalo. The people that lived there with them were content, and they shared a mutual respect so the buffalo were not threatened by these inhabitants. Some years went by and there was talk about pale-skins immigrating towards them. With this, many council meetings were held and much discussion was made on what will be done, for they also learned that their people were ailing and that the animals of the areas were frightened and running. One of the Elders, Medicine Man Manysmartmoves, felt that his Nation and the buffalo could be upset by this. So for four nights Manysmartmoves went into the hills where the buffalo roamed, and he prayed to the Creator. A vision came to him on the third night. As he lay there, the wind started to blow and the buffalo that were standing near him started to bend and sway with the power of the wind. Then in front of him a bright green plant grew and turned to dust. Exhausted and thankful, the Medicine Man Manysmartmoves prayed for the last day and night, thanking the Great Spirit for the gift received. He headed back to where the people were waiting for him to find out what they were to do. The Medicine Man called a council meeting and announced that he was to go back into the hills with the buffalo to protect their sacredness. He was told by the

Great Spirit that these pale-skinned peoples do not understand the importance of respecting Mother Earth and everything on her. He told them that his vision was to turn the buffalo into the Standing People until the time comes that they can live free again. The San Pueblo Nation took on this heavy decision and went to their homes and prayed for the generations ahead and for the strength of Mother Earth. That night Manysmartmoves went to the buffalo and prayed for their sacrifice. He then fed the stream where they drank the dust of the bright green plant. Over a span of seven months where the buffalo once stood were now full green trees.

Now as you drive through New Mexico and the hills are covered with stocky, full trees remember that these were once four-legged and sacrificed their existence then for another beginning. We can aide in their return by believing in ourselves and that everything around us has emotion and Spirit.

Mahsi cho

Aboriginal Day

I saw you, watched you, pretending you watched me in the same sort of way. I saw you at a drum dance in Dettah, your jacket was so beautiful, probably sewn for you. Beaded every thoughtful bead by your one true love, worn with humble pride.

Saw you again much later. You were talking to people. You've really grown, doing great things.

I'm honoured, that's what I enjoy, admire, that we are not as lost as I sometimes think we are. That we are moving for the better, the traditional, the cherished.

You drum and sing, we are watching you… you are shining.

Global Warming

Hey world. Today I am here. Living. Being.
Acknowledged. Recognized. Here.
A little worse for wear at times but still shining.
Pining. Sometimes whining.

Hello world. I'm writing again. Been awhile.
But still smile. Beguile. Rile.
Going to find out if this story is worth telling.
Soon.

Hi world. Visited you today. Got to one of your
    warmer areas where I've never been.
Swam in your waters daily. Had to. It was hot there.
Saw beautiful colours there. Like I have never seen.
Such rich teal, aquamarine waters.
Thank you world for your beauty.

World! Back home again. Here. In the North.
The weather is a little mild for my liking.
I'm getting a little concerned.
Perhaps world it is the end of you soon.

Familial Retribution

1.

A boy watched a man fall
He closed his eyes and can't recall
Memories still cloud his view.

She fell in love with a crooked kin
Who couldn't give her all of him
It still hurts sometimes to see.

But when all the rain stopped crying
When all the wind stopped trying to knock them down
They saw each other and knew there might still be one
more chance.

He wiped the dust off the mirror that had gathered there
for years
He looked to see where he was
She stood there beside him and saw the man he had yet
to become.

She's one foot on land and the other over there
She believes she is. So she becomes.
But today she sees her infallibility and still doesn't
believe it.

2.

A widowed son
A martyred man reminded by his eldest
A replicate
A black sheep brother left to pasture by his mother
Turned around many times by his passions and desires
Fell in love once or twice
Fell harder for the bottle, the rolled and the snort
Kept his head above water except when he drowned
And rarely let his feet touch the ground
Remembers every incident like a stab wound
Recalls it with the same fury as the first
There is no pain like self-objectivity
There is no discipline than that which comes from self
There is no wickedness worse than righteousness.

3.

A tall Métis man
Identified by dark brown hair and hazel eyes
His nose a family original and his lips are hers.
I wish the demons better luck
To rush a man whose life is lived by getting stuck
There is not much they can do
Walking with only one shoe
Unless they are willing to walk with the wounded
With both of one far from the other
He is a balanced extremist
Trapped in a sidewalk world.

4.

A forgotten daughter
A defeated man reminded by his eldest replicate
A black sheep sister left to pasture by her others
Turned around many times by her passions and desires
Fell in love once or twice
Fell harder for the lusted, the one-night, the sport
Kept her head above water except when she drowned
And occasionally let her feet touch the ground
Recalls every incident like a flesh-coloured scar
Caressing it with the remembered fury it once possessed
The truth always reveals itself
Loves core is trust
There is no pain like objectivity.

5.

A petite Northern woman,
Dark brown hair and "hazel" eyes
Her nose, a family original and her lips are his
I wish the demons better pay
To rush a woman whose life is lived by going astray
There is not much they can do
Following a runaway
Unless they are willing to walk with the wounded
With both of one and seeing the other
She is a walking contradiction
With a weakness for the misguided.

6.

A widowed son and a forgotten daughter
Fell in love one last time
Cherishing each moment like it's their last
Every revealed wound is eventually healed
There never was a castle built on sand that stood the test of time
With change comes growth
With love comes freedom
And there are no demons here.

Haiku

1.

senses rush
I Love You
red lips glisten

2.

opposite of dull
this ache flows like needles
my body warm with hurt

3.

your beauty
how it shows roughly
like a miner looking for gold

Thoughts and Other Human Tendencies

I sat upon my windowsill
Wondering if you love me still?

...Saw the centre of a gun...

I still consider death.

Gazing on and off
towards you and your innocent outlook
on the complexity of woman oh, excuse me,
women.

I wish I had a travelling guitar.
I wish that you weren't so far away.
The world divide in space collide.

Open thoughts.
are they profound?
all this pain for what!

"I heard in Mexico you can buy a bottle of wine for a dollar."

Spoken by a drunken man on Gold Range Street to his drunken pal

"I don't believe in God. I believe in Aliens."

A fellow from San Diego, "Tony," in Bob's Youth Hostel – Amsterdam

Followed my taste buds, then thought of you.

As I sit here in the land of Daisy Dreams…

An old man builds his house at 71
Finds his home, his heart
and sets up camp.

"Bananas soy
strawberries and blue
regular moo."
Guy waiter in Macy's Flagstaff referring to my oatmeal

Food is commercialized like our personalities,
A product that sells fast, appearance is everything.
How fast can you look good,
How fast can you eat?

Are cell phones a slow suicide?

"Money cannot augment what is truly human."
Spoken by someone close at a better moment in our lives

...Must you believe what I wear...

Sucks to be a sucker in a pinstriped suit.

"Only after the last tree has been cut down,
Only after the last river has been poisoned,
Only after the last fish has been caught,
Only then will you find that money cannot be eaten."
Cree Indian Prophecy

Sweet talker says cold harsh words
into my ears as he enters me
like the reversal of a baby being born.

Am I more good than bad?

…I thought the world was my oyster…
…I thought my name was real…

Love passing through the cracks of sidewalks
With every step I take, a piece of me is falling down.

Safety net can withstand whatever it is given.
Where is yours?
And, will it catch me?

Compromise is the beginning of death,
Regret bouncing in your head
Reacting to later events.
Making itself the man invited to every party.

"I have to find my inspiration."
"Have another drink, you'll find it."
Youth Hostel in Paris
Guy from Quebec playing harmonica stops, and an American guy responds

Sometimes we think we are,
And we learn at times we are not.
It is unusual this pendulum from which we swing.

Perhaps it's not about ego
but that innate desire to tell a story
and stories can only be told.

Perhaps if I were to synchronize my watch to the rapid beat of your soul.
I then would be able to enhance my pleasure of being with you.

I am tired of being labelled.
But, do I always want to be adored?
Sometimes I don't want to be labelled.
Sometimes I want to be ignored.

Did I miss something here?
Besides me missing you.
or
Is there something I'm missing besides you?

Ruining tonight, missing you.
I apologize for my inability to feel
You probably didn't notice it, but I felt it.
Tears, like rain, drop.

"Where I'm going,
Is not going anywhere."
Antoine Mountain standing on a street corner
enjoying good conversation

I can't hear tomorrow when yesterday are cotton balls
in my ears.

If I ever knew the game: and if I played it well, I never
knew…
I guess you can say it was blind passion, lost focus,
non-incidental actions.
I was here and we played well together.

In every tomb
There is a man who loved you.

Compromise is the poor man's power.

I once asked a boy if he understood the meaning of life.
He replied, "Yes, it's when your toy has been bought,
and knowing it's yours to keep."

Crows play in the wind. Like children in the sand.

"Many years ago… when the rocks were soft."
Robbie Romero

Sitting here, all of us, with pen, with paper.
We are all writers. We all have deep sorrow.

Life has led me down many roads
Do you hitchhike too?

What do I want?
Where do I want to go… besides to the top.
Ha ha ha.

Dark, bitter-tasting sanity hurts my muscles.

Insomnia = In need of something and can't sleep until
it is found.

My Haunted Hunted Heart.

If I could stand there looking in your eyes
long enough to not want to close mine
then perhaps then it would be love.

FiNe.

Acknowledgements

The people and places that have inspired *Thoughts and Other Human Tendencies* are vast though I wouldn't have written this book if it weren't for my family. This is for my mother, Suzan Marie, and brother, Chris Marie, and for Grandma and Grandpa Archie whose courage, strength and awareness of the world taught me to be fearless with an open heart and have an adventurous spirit.

I'd like to acknowledge the lovers that spurned me, turned me on and fell for me too, ultimately these words are for you. I'd like to give thanks to the land that holds my footsteps and feeds my eyes with its beauty, these words are for you. I'd like to acknowledge the people whose words captured me and just had to be shared with others besides me.

I'd like to acknowledge BookLand Press for giving these words shape and an audience, thank you. To my friends whose love and support allow me to fly without boundaries and keep me humble with grounded joy. Mahsi cho.